This book belongs to

_ _ _ _ _ _ _ _ _ _ _ _ _ _ _

BE NICE.
ROLL DICE.

"Great game!" I told my friend.

I so badly wanted to win the race, but knew that I had given it my best try. I reminded myself that there would be many more opportunities in the future.

Being a good sport didn't come naturally to me. I've learned to practice good sportsmanship even when I'm feeling disappointed.

For instance...

Whenever I get behind in a game, I continue to play by the rules.

On the playground when my friends ask me to play kickball,
I agree even though I might not be very good at it.

I haven't always known how to deal with disappointment.

Each time I became disappointed, I wanted to quit, cheat, or cry.

For example, if I was losing a game, I wanted to stop playing even though we were in the middle of a game.

When my friend forgot the score, I would cheat and lie about it so I could win.

And if my team lost, I didn't want to shake our opponents' hands.

How did I learn how to deal with disappointment, you ask?

Well, let me explain...

One day during a game against Growth Mindset Ninja, I decided to stop trying since I was losing.

Growth Mindset Ninja pulled out some dice from a pocket.

These are called Good Sportsmanship Dice. There are six sides representing six different good sportsmanship strategies you can use:

Remind yourself that it's just a game and say "I can always try again."

Handshake and tell the winner, "Great job!"

Tell your partner, "Great try" after missing a shot.

An easy way to remember this is Be Nice, Roll Dice.

The next day was Field Day.

It was a good thing I had just learned those strategies from the Good Sportsmanship Dice because I quickly put them to use!

I encouraged my teammates when we were losing.

Great job!

I tried my best even though I got behind.

I was able to deal with disappointment much better from that day forward.

And everyone liked the good sportsmanship I displayed. Better yet, I liked it, too!

Remembering the strategies in the Good Sportsmanship Dice could be your secret weapon in building your good sportsmanship superpower!

Please download your Good Sportsmanship Dice Activity and check out our beyond the book resources at ninjalifehacks.tv

@marynhin @GrowGrit
#NinjaLifeHacks

Mary Nhin Ninja Life Hacks

Ninja Life Hacks

Keep playing even though you are losing.

Take deep breaths.

Play fair, no cheating.

Made in the USA
Las Vegas, NV
10 October 2023